A NOTE TO PARENTS

Reading Aloud with Your Child

Research shows that reading books aloud is the single most valuable support parents can provide in helping children learn to read.

- Be a ham! The more enthusiasm you display, the more your child will enjoy the book.
- Run your finger underneath the words as you read to signal that the print carries the story.
- Leave time for examining the illustrations more closely; encourage your child to find things in the pictures.
- Invite your youngster to join in whenever there's a repeated phrase in the text.
- Link up events in the book with similar events in your child's life.
- If your child asks a question, stop and answer it. The book can be a means to learning more about your child's thoughts.

Listening to Your Child Read Aloud

The support of your attention and praise is absolutely crucial to your child's continuing efforts to learn to read.

- If your child is learning to read and asks for a word, give it immediately so that the meaning of the story is not interrupted. DO NOT ask your child to sound out the word.
- On the other hand, if your child initiates the act of sounding out, don't intervene.
- If your child is reading along and makes what is called a miscue, listen for the sense of the miscue. If the word "road" is substituted for the word "street," for instance, no meaning is lost. Don't stop the reading for a correction.
- If the miscue makes no sense (for example, "horse" for "house"), ask your child to reread the sentence because you're not sure you understand what's just been read.
- Above all else, enjoy your child's growing command of print and make sure you give lots of praise. *You are your child's first teacher — and the most important one. Praise from you is critical for further risk-taking and learning.*

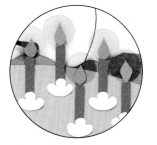

— Priscilla Lynch
Ph.D., New York University
Educational Consultant

Crete Park
Pre - School

To brave firefighters everywhere
—J. Marzollo

For Maddie and Andy
—J. Moffatt

Text copyright © 1996 by Jean Marzollo
Illustrations copyright © 1996 by Judith Moffatt
All rights reserved. Published by Scholastic Inc.
HELLO READER!, CARTWHEEL BOOKS, and the CARTWHEEL BOOKS logo
are registered trademarks of Scholastic Inc.

Library of Congress Cataloging-in-Publication Data

Marzollo, Jean.
    I am fire / by Jean Marzollo ; illustrated by Judith Moffatt.
        p.   cm. — (Hello reader! Level 1)
    Summary: Explains the difference between good fire, which can be used safely for cooking and providing warmth, and bad fire, which can cause burns or destroy property.
    ISBN 0-590-84778-3
    1. Fire prevention — Juvenile literature. 2. Fire — Juvenile literature.
[1. Fire. 2. Fire prevention. 3. Safety.]
I. Moffatt, Judith, ill.   II. Title.   III. Series.
TH9148.M32   1996
628.9'2 — dc20   95-25750
                                                                              CIP
                                                                               AC

12 11 10 9 8 7 6 5 4 3 2 1   6 7 8 9/9 0 1/0
                        Printed in the U.S.A.   24
            First Scholastic printing, September 1996

I Am Fire

by Jean Marzollo
Illustrated by Judith Moffatt

Hello Science Reader! — Level 1

SCHOLASTIC INC.
New York   Toronto   London   Auckland   Sydney

Fire heats your soup.

Fire warms your rooms.

Fire lights your life.

But watch out!
Fire can be harmful.

Children can help to
prevent fires.
If you find matches,
give them to a grown-up.
Do not try to light them.

Watch fireworks with a grown-up. Stay way back.

Fire is hot.
Don't touch fire.
Don't touch hot things.
Just look.

Practice fire drills
at home.

Have a place to meet.

Practice fire drills
at school, too.

If you see a fire start,
tell a grown-up quickly.

If you are inside a building
that's on fire, go out.

If there is smoke, crawl under it. Stay low and go. Don't go back inside.

If your clothes are on fire,
stop where you are.
Drop to the ground.
Roll over and over to smother
the flames.
Remember these three words.
Stop. Drop. Roll.

If you want to know more about fire, ask a grown-up.

Learn how to call the fire department where you live.